942.021

THE HISTORY DETECTIVE

INVESTIGATES

The Normans and the Battle of Hastings

Philip Parker

WAYLAND

First published in 2010 by Wayland

Wayland
338 Euston Road
London NW1 3BH

Wayland Australia
Level 17/207 Kent Street
Sydney, NSW 2000

Editor: David John
Designer: Darren Jordan
Consultant: Andy Robertshaw

British Library Cataloguing in Publication Data:
Parker, Philip.
   Normans and the Battle of Hastings. -- (The history
detective investigates)
   1. Hastings, Battle of, England, 1066--Juvenile
literature. 2. Great Britain--History--Norman period,
1066-1154--Juvenile literature.
   I. Title II. Series
942'.021-dc22

ISBN: 978-0-7502-6228-6

Printed in China

Wayland is a division of Hachette Children's Books,
an Hachette UK company

This replica of a Norman helmet shows the long metal tab that protected the wearer's nose.

Contents

Words in **bold** can be found in the glossary on page 30.

 The history detective Sherlock Bones will help you to find clues and collect evidence about the Normans and the Battle of Hastings. Wherever you see one of Sherlock's paw-prints, you will find a mystery to solve. The answers can be found on page 31.

Who were the Normans?

The Normans became powerful in northern France more than a thousand years ago. When they invaded England in the year 1066, they dramatically changed the history of our country, bringing their own styles of building, art and warfare. They still influence us today.

The Norman people had not always lived in France. They came originally from Scandinavia (modern-day Denmark, Sweden and Norway) and were part of a group of people known as the Vikings. From about 800 to 1000, the Vikings raided rich towns and monasteries along the coasts of Britain, Ireland and France in search of gold and slaves. The French called them 'Northmen', which later became 'Normans'.

In 911, a group of Vikings led by Hrolf attacked the French town of Rouen. The French king, Charles the Simple, was impressed by Hrolf. He made an agreement with Hrolf's Vikings. In return for lands around Rouen, Hrolf's Viking group would defend France against other Viking bands.

Hrolf was given the title of **count** and was known afterwards as Count Rollo (the French version of his name). In the years that followed, the Normans took more and more land until they controlled most of modern Normandy. They soon turned their backs on the old Viking gods and became Christians. To demonstrate their new faith, they built great stone churches, such as the one at Jumièges, which was the most important in Normandy. Over time, the Normans intermarried with their French neighbours. They began to speak French, too, instead of their old Scandinavian language, which died out.

DETECTIVE WORK

Although it's now a ruin, the famous abbey at Jumièges shows us how important the Normans' Christian faith was to them. Find out more about the abbey's history at http://en.wikipedia.org/wiki/Jumièges_Abbey

The Vikings crossed the North Sea from Scandinavia in warships, terrorising the coasts of France and England. The French king gave them land in northern France in return for protection.

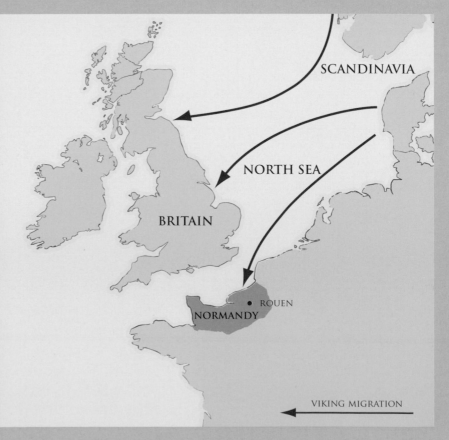

SCANDINAVIA

NORTH SEA

BRITAIN

ROUEN

NORMANDY

VIKING MIGRATION

In the ninth century, the 'Northmen' burnt the abbey at Jumièges to the ground, but they had built an even larger one to replace it by 1067.

'If the Normans are disciplined under a just and firm rule, they are men of great valour… But without such rule they tear each other to pieces and destroy themselves, for they hanker after rebellion, cherish sedition, and are ready for any treachery.'

English chronicler Orderic Vitalis, writing in *Ecclesiastical History* (**circa** 1114–41)

By the end of the tenth century, the ruler of Normandy was known as a duke – the highest rank below a king. The lands of a duke are known as a duchy, and Normandy became one of the most powerful duchies in Europe. The Normans became famous for their fighting spirit and strong Christian beliefs. Their armies crossed the Mediterranean Sea and set up Norman kingdoms in Sicily and southern Italy. They also set off on **crusades** to capture the Holy Lands of the Bible from Muslim rulers in the Near East (modern-day Syria, Lebanon and Israel). But it was in their **conquest** of England that they had the biggest impact on history.

Norman knights were armed with a sword, a dagger and sometimes a **mace** (a type of club).

Apart from his chain mail coat, what other protection does this knight have?

Who was Duke William of Normandy?

In 1035, a seven-year-old boy called **William** became the duke of Normandy. His father, Robert II, had died while returning from a **pilgrimage**. William was much too young to rule by himself, so a series of guardians ruled for him until he was 15. Although he was young, William soon became the greatest of all the Normans.

William was an impressive young man. He was healthy, tall and fair, with arms so powerful he could shoot an arrow while riding his horse at full gallop. He also had a strong personality and could attract the support of his people.

But William's power in Normandy was not secure. He faced threats of **rebellion** and invasion. However, by the time he was 19 he was successfully fighting off his enemies. The king of France, Henry I, was so worried about the growing power of Normandy that he twice tried to invade William's lands. Both times William defeated him.

DETECTIVE WORK

When William was born it was not certain that he would follow his father to become the duke of Normandy. This was because William's father and mother were not married. William's mother was said to come from a lowly background. Find out who she was on http://en.wikipedia.org/wiki/Herleva

William was born in this castle at Falaise, near Calvados, in Normandy.

In his struggle against Normandy's enemies, William received help from many **noble** Norman families, such as the Beaumonts and Montgomeries, whose members later went with him to England and became great Anglo-Norman aristocrats. He was also helped by his half-brother, Odo of Bayeux, who became a famous bishop.

By about 1060, William's position in Normandy was much stronger. He was a very active and driven man. His main enemies, including King Henry I of France, had died, and the new king of France, Philip I, was just eight years old. William now felt strong enough to begin enlarging Normandy's territory and increasing Norman power.

This is a scene from the famous Bayeux Tapestry, which records many details of life in Norman times. William (centre) is shown passing judgement on a prisoner.

'From this time William began with the utmost zeal to protect the churches of God, to uphold the cause of the weak, to impose laws which would not be burdensome, and to make judgements which never deviated from equity and temperance. He especially prohibited slaughter, fire and pillage.'

William of Poitiers writing in *Gesta Gulielmi*, a book about the life of William of Normandy (c.1071–77)

This penny coin was made after William became king of England, so everyone in the country would see the face of their ruler.

🐾 **On the coin, William wears a crown. What does he hold in front of his face?**

Why did the Normans want to invade England?

William had become a confident, energetic and successful ruler. Now that he was secure in Normandy, he began to think about the rich lands across the Channel in England.

The king of England, Edward the Confessor, had ruled England since 1042. But Edward had spent more than 20 years living as an **exile** in Normandy after his father, King Aethelred, had been **overthrown** by the Vikings. Edward was also William's first cousin, and the two men knew each other well. William probably visited Edward in London in 1051. Later, William claimed that Edward had promised him the English throne. Many English nobles did not believe this. Whether it was true or not, William became very interested in England.

In the summer of 1064, Harold Godwinson, the earl of Wessex and the most powerful man in England after the king, sailed to Normandy. Nobody is quite sure what the reason for Harold's mission was, but it may have been to ask for the release of his brother, who was being held **hostage** in Normandy. Harold's ship, however, was driven by a storm into the lands of Count Guy of Ponthieu, who arrested Harold.

'Harold swore fealty to him... And... at the crucial point in the oath he... pronounced these words, that as long as he lived he would be the vicar of Duke William... that he would strive to the utmost... to ensure that the English monarchy should be pledged to him after Edward's death.'

William of Poitiers writing in *Gesta Gulielmi*

King Edward the Confessor (centre) is shown in this famous portrait known as the *Wilton Diptych*. It was painted in about 1395.

Harold would have crossed the Channel to Normandy in a longship similar to those of the Vikings.

Duke William, hearing of this, forced Guy to release Harold and invited him to stay at his castle in Normandy as his guest. In return for the favours William showed him, Harold swore an **oath** to the Norman duke. The Normans saw this as **fealty**, a sign that Harold was now William's man and would help William become king of England if called upon to do so. Harold did not see it that way, but this oath gave William an extra reason to claim the English throne if the chance arose.

Harold got to know William well. He fought alongside him in Normandy, and gained first-hand experience of Norman battle tactics. When Harold finally returned home to England, he was not aware that the oath that he had sworn to William would one day come back to haunt him, or that the two of them would become bitter enemies. They would not meet again until they were face to face on the battlefield.

DETECTIVE WORK

Some of what we know about Edward the Confessor comes from a very old book called the *Anglo-Saxon Chronicle*. This book was begun by a famous English king. Find out who it was. Why was he known as 'the Great'?

🐾 In the picture below, Harold (centre) is touching a type of box. What do you think it might be?

In this detail of the Bayeux Tapestry, Harold is shown swearing fealty to William.

UBI HAROLD:SACRAMENTUM:FECIT:⁂ hIC HAROLD:DUX
VVILLELMO DUCI:⁖

Who were the Anglo-Saxons?

The people of England at the time of William of Normandy were called Anglo-Saxons. In the fifth century, groups of warlike German tribes known as Jutes, Angles and Saxons started to cross over the North Sea to England. Gradually they pushed the native British people westwards to Wales and Cornwall, and northwards to Scotland. The new arrivals set up their own kingdoms, and by the ninth century, the strongest of these was Wessex, which controlled almost all of England. The Anglo-Saxons had a rich tradition of reciting poetry and stories. They were also skilled in metalwork and making jewellery.

While William was ruling Normandy, England was ruled by King Edward the Confessor. When Edward came to the throne in 1042, he faced many problems controlling the Anglo-Saxon **earls**, who held the real power in large areas of the kingdom.

'In their days Hengest and Horsa, invited by Vortigern, king of the Britons... described the worthlessness of the Britons, and the richness of the land. They [the Angles] then sent them greater support. Then came the men from three powers of Germany; the Old Saxons, the Angles, and the Jutes.'

The *Anglo-Saxon Chronicle*

Corfe Castle in Dorset (above) is the site of an Anglo-Saxon fort. It was rebuilt in stone after the Norman Conquest.

This is a reconstruction of a ceremonial Anglo-Saxon helmet found buried at Sutton Hoo in Suffolk.

This fine gold clasp would have held an Anglo-Saxon cloak in place.

Edward tried to stop them becoming too strong by giving important jobs in England to Normans, rather than the earls. Edward had strong links to Normandy because he had lived in exile there.

The Normans that lived in England were not popular with the earls, and in 1051 Earl Godwin of Wessex rebelled against the king. Although he was defeated and sent into exile, Godwin returned with an army in 1052 and forced Edward to send away his Norman advisers.

In 1053, Earl Godwin died and his son, Harold Godwinson, became the earl of Wessex. Harold served King Edward the Confessor loyally. It seemed unlikely that Harold would ever become king himself. But when Edward fell seriously ill in 1065, Edward's great-nephew and **heir** to the English throne was only 14 years old. So Harold acted quickly. He married the sister of Earl Edwin of Mercia and Earl Morcar of Northumbria, who were his only serious rivals. When Edward died on 5 January 1066, the council of royal advisers, known as the Witan, chose Harold to be the next king of England. He was crowned the following day at Westminster Abbey, and, with all the earls supporting him, it looked as though he might **reign** for a long time. In fact he reigned for only nine months.

🐾 **Why do you think Anglo-Saxon nobles were buried with their gold and valuables?**

DETECTIVE WORK

One of the most famous Anglo-Saxon stories is about a hero defeating a horrible monster called Grendel who had been attacking an imaginary kingdom. What was the name of the story? This story would have been told aloud to entertain people. Try reciting the story to your family or friends.

What was life like in England in the year 1066?

Over time, England changed a lot from the early years of Anglo-Saxon rule. By 1066 the country was unified under the kings of Wessex, and the threat from Viking invaders was over. But life was still hard for ordinary people.

Most of the people of Anglo-Saxon England lived in small villages and on farms. They were known as *ceorls*. They laboured on the land or they were craftsmen, and they had the right to give their land to their heirs (or to sell it) if they wanted to. As time went on, the *ceorls* had to pay the local lord a share of their produce or do a fixed number of days' work on his estate.

DETECTIVE WORK

Oxford or Winchester are very ancient cities so it seems strange to think of a time when they were new and planned. Find out what other cities in England were built as *burhs* in the time of the Anglo-Saxons on http://www.britainexpress.com/architecture/burhs.htm

There are about 50 Anglo-Saxon churches left in Britain. Some are built with stone reused from Roman buildings.

In 1066, Anglo-Saxon towns were thriving. During the reign of King Alfred the Great (who ruled Wessex from 871 to 899) England faced great danger from Viking invaders. To defend Wessex against the Vikings, Alfred set up a system of *burhs* – towns with fortress walls around them. Landowners had to provide money and men to support these new towns. Some, such as Oxford and Winchester, attracted tradesmen and merchants. As a result, town populations increased. However, they were small by modern standards: Oxford had about 3,000 inhabitants, and London about 12,000.

Anglo-Saxon houses were made of wood with straw roofs. Only churches were built of stone.

Most people in Anglo-Saxon England could not read or write. Only monks or priests could read, and they did so in Latin, not in Anglo-Saxon. King Alfred the Great had encouraged monks to translate some books from Latin into Anglo-Saxon, but libraries with lots of books were found only in **monasteries**.

Anglo-Saxon peasants sometimes cooked inside their huts and sometimes outside. When did they cook inside the hut and why?

The Anglo-Saxon nobles were called *thegns* (pronounced 'thanes'). They lived in manor houses surrounded by the lands of the peasants who owed them labour service. Some of the most important *thegns* became powerful earls.

Ordinary people would see an earl only on rare occasions. Their contact with the government was through the *shire-reeve* (or sheriff) who was in charge of the local courts where justice was given.

An Anglo-Saxon peasant knocks down acorns for his boars to eat.

What threats did the Anglo-Saxons face?

Harold Godwinson's reign was brief but action-packed. He had only been king of England for a few months when he received some alarming news. A force of invaders had landed in the north of England, and Harold's own brother, Tostig, the earl of Northumbria, was with them.

The invaders were led by Harald Hardrada, the king of Norway. He believed the English throne should be his. In the summer of 1066, Harold Godwinson's brother Tostig had escaped to Norway when the people of Northumbria rebelled against his harsh rule. With such an important earl as Tostig on his side, Harald Hardrada decided to invade England, and in autumn 1066 set sail for England with 300 ships. They landed at Riccall in Yorkshire. The invaders then defeated the local Anglo-Saxon forces just south of York, at Fulford.

Harold Godwinson reached the area of York with a large army just four days after the Battle of Fulford. Harald Hardrada was caught by surprise and, at Stamford Bridge on 25 September, a bloody battle ended with the total defeat of the Norwegians.

'The closer the army came, the greater it grew, and their glittering weapons sparkled like a field of broken ice.'

Icelandic historian Snorri Sturluson on the approach of Harold Godwinson's army to York (c.1230)

DETECTIVE WORK

Harald Hardrada thought he would get support in northern England because York used to be a stronghold of the Vikings. Find out the Viking name for York. What was the name of the most famous Viking ruler of York?

What were the wooden heads on the Viking ships?

The Norwegians arrived in 300 ships (reconstructed here), but so few survived the battle that they needed only 24 ships to sail home.

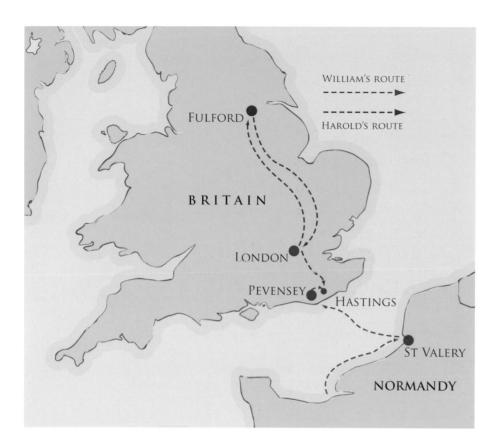

This map shows Harold's race northward to Yorkshire, and then southward to face William.

The Battle of Fulford was mostly fought hand to hand. Few horses were used.

Both Harald Hardrada and Tostig were killed. But Harold Godwinson was not safe yet. Soon after the battle, he heard even more worrying news – that William of Normandy had set sail from France with a large army.

Harold Godwinson turned his army around and began the long march back south to face this new threat. By 8 October he had reached London, and, after a pause to gather more men, he moved southeast to Hastings, where William had set up his headquarters.

The Norman army had landed at Pevensey in Sussex on 29 September and at once built a wooden castle there. The Normans were not very secure on the English coast. They were far from home and without proper supplies. Although his own army was tired, Harold Godwinson believed that, if he could defeat the Normans quickly, he would be able to drive them out of England.

What happened in the Battle of Hastings?

The Battle of Hastings is one of the most important battles in English history. It was a complete victory for the Normans, and marked the end of Anglo-Saxon power in England. But on the day of the battle it was not obvious who would win...

By 13 October, Harold was very close to Hastings. His army was about 8,000 strong and he positioned it to prevent the Normans — whose force was probably about the same size — from breaking out and advancing towards London. At dawn on 14 October, William sent his men forward. The Anglo-Saxons had taken up position on top of a hill called Senlac, and they formed a dense wall by **interlocking** their shields together. This made it difficult for the Normans, who had to struggle up the steep slope, to penetrate the Anglo-Saxon line.

Later that morning, the Normans sent a thick rain of arrows into the Anglo-Saxon ranks, then attacked on foot, but were beaten back. Next, the Norman **cavalry** moved up the hill, but they failed to break the shield wall. Some of William's men began to run away and a rumour spread that William had been killed. Some Anglo-Saxons left the hill to attack the escaping troops, but were surrounded and cut down.

DETECTIVE WORK

In the very last stages of the Battle of Hastings, many Norman knights were killed by the Anglo-Saxons as their horses fell into a deep ditch. Can you find out what it was called? Why do you think William chose Christmas Day to be crowned king?

Why are the archers shooting up into the air instead of aiming at a target?

The battle opens with a dense volley of Norman arrows, followed by a cavalry charge.

William **rallied** his troops and at about midday changed his tactic. He ordered a series of feigned (pretend) retreats, to try to tempt the Anglo-Saxons once more off the hill. This tactic was only partly successful. The main Anglo-Saxon line of shields held firm. William then ordered his archers to shoot another rain of arrows and it seems that one of these may have hit Harold in the eye, wounding him badly. News of this spread and some Anglo-Saxons retreated, allowing the Normans to storm the top of the hill. By this time, Harold had died, along with two of his brothers. Harold's elite force, the *huscarls*, made a brave last stand on Senlac Hill, but most of them were killed.

William stayed for a week around Hastings and then marched on London. Within a few weeks, most of the leading Anglo-Saxon nobles had surrendered, been captured or become loyal to William. On Christmas Day 1066, in Westminster Abbey, William was crowned king of England.

The two sides fight in a bloody, face-to-face battle.

'*The king who was the glory of the realm, the darling of the clergy, the strength of his soldiers, the shield of the defenceless… the pearl of princes, was slain by his fierce foe.*'

The *Waltham Chronicle* on the death of Harold Godwinson

'*The Normans, suddenly wheeling round their horses, checked and encircled them, and slaughtered them to the last man.*'

William of Poitiers writing in *Gesta Gulielmi*

The Bayeux Tapestry is said to show the moment Harold (on the right) is hit.

What weapons were used in the battle?

The two sides in the **Battle of Hastings** were not like modern armies. Apart from the arrows of the Norman archers, shot from a distance away, most of the fighting took place face to face, with heavy swords, axes, lances, shields and daggers. It was noisy, chaotic and very bloody.

On the Anglo-Saxon side, there were not many professional soldiers. Most of them were ordinary farmers. They were given weapons by the big landowners. The number of men the landowners supplied depended on the size of their estates. These soldiers were responsible for defending local areas against raiders, and were known as the *fyrd*. If there was a national emergency, they could serve outside their home counties and more men might be called up, but those would be less well trained and armed.

DETECTIVE WORK

Even though the Normans were fighting uphill, they had two things that gave them a big advantage over Harold's army – cavalry and archers. Why do you think these gave William such an advantage? Imagine the beginning of the battle before the hand-to-hand fighting started.

This is a selection of replica weapons used in the battle. *Fyrd* without swords fought with farmers' tools.

The Anglo-Saxon king's bodyguard, the *huscarls*, were much better trained than the *fyrd*. They wore leather armour with iron rings sewn into it (called chain mail) and pointed steel helmets with long nose-guards. They carried large wooden shields and long battle-axes. A soldier in the *fyrd* normally had worse equipment than this, with only a leather shirt (and no iron rings), a small round shield and a variety of weapons, such as the seax (a long dagger), a spear and a small axe. There were also a few archers in the Anglo-Saxon army, but very little cavalry.

The Norman side probably had better weapons. The Norman knights were more like professional soldiers and many of them had experience of fighting, from Duke William's long wars to become ruler of Normandy. Because they fought on horseback, they could ride at foot soldiers in a devastating **charge**.

Norman knights wore coats of chain mail similar to those of the Anglo-Saxon *huscarls*. Beneath this they wore a protective padded under-coat as a cushion against blows and to prevent the iron rings being driven into the wearer's body by an enemy's sword-thrust. The Norman chain mail was slashed at the front and back to allow its wearer to ride on horseback. Normans, too, wore pointed metal helmets. The Norman knights carried long spears or javelins to thrust at enemies as they charged. They also carried swords. Some of the Normans – including Bishop Odo of Bayeux – are shown in the Bayeux Tapestry carrying a mace or a club. The Normans had far more archers than the Anglo-Saxons and could use these from a distance to strike at the Anglo-Saxon army.

The Anglo-Saxon *fyrd* used small, rounded shields similar to those of the Vikings.

Chain mail took a long time to make. Each ring had to be linked with a hammer.

🐾 **Do you think arrows could penetrate chain mail?**

What does the Bayeux Tapestry tell us about the battle?

The Bayeux Tapestry is an amazing piece of embroidery nearly 70 m (230 ft) long. It uses pictures to tell the story of the **Norman Conquest**, beginning in 1064. It ends with the defeat of King Harold by William of Normandy at Hastings.

There are 58 separate scenes, and many of them have writing in Latin to explain the action. The tapestry might have been ordered by Bishop Odo of Bayeux, but there is no real evidence for this. No one is quite sure when it was made, or where.

Because the tapestry may have been woven within a few decades of the Battle of Hastings, it gives us a good idea of what people at the time believed had happened in the battle. It does not tell the whole story of 1066, however, because the invasion of Harald Hardrada and the Battle of Stamford Bridge are missed out completely.

🐾 **In the scene below, what are Harold's men doing with their shields?**

This part of the tapestry shows the thick of the fighting.

Bishop Odo of Bayeux is seen here fighting with a mace.

DETECTIVE WORK

In one scene of the tapestry, a comet is shown in the sky. We know this comet appeared in 1066 because it passes the Earth every 76 years. Find out the name of this comet. How old will you be when it next appears in our skies?

Some episodes shown in the tapestry, such as Harold's visit to Normandy in 1064 and the appearance of a comet in the sky in 1066, are also mentioned in other sources of evidence from the time. This means that much of what is shown on the tapestry is probably near the truth. The battle itself is shown in the final eight scenes of the tapestry. Episodes such as the Norman attacks on the Anglo-Saxon shield wall, the false retreat by the Normans and their turning on the Anglo-Saxons and cutting them down, are all pictured, as is the death of Harold and the final escape of the remaining Anglo-Saxons.

'Item: a very long and narrow strip of linen, embroidered with figures and inscription representing the Conquest of England, which is hung round the nave of the church on the Feast of Relics and throughout the Octave.'

From an inventory of the Church of Notre-Dame of Bayeux, 1476 – the first definite mention of the Bayeux Tapestry

As well as showing us what went on in 1066, the Bayeux Tapestry is also a vital source of evidence for the types of clothes the Anglo-Saxons and Normans wore, and the weapons they carried into battle. It even shows us what some buildings (such as Westminster Abbey, which was built in 1065) looked like.

Here the tapestry shows the surviving Anglo-Saxons running away.

What was England like under Norman rule?

Although he had won the Battle of Hastings, William did not conquer the rest of England so easily. Many parts of the country fought hard against him. To become the true ruler of England, William acted cruelly. From 1067 to 1072 he crushed a series of **revolts** and gave orders for the remaining Anglo-Saxon nobles to be killed or to have their lands taken from them.

William began building a great number of castles to keep the country under control. Norman nobles were given vast areas of territory, and the king kept for himself a fifth of the total agricultural land of the country. Large numbers of *fiefs* were created. These were estates held by a lord who owed service directly to the king. The lord had **vassals** who owed him service, including workers who lived on his estate. This is called the **feudal system**, and it lasted for centuries in England.

DETECTIVE WORK

After William became king of England, he and his descendants continued to rule Normandy for more than 100 years. But in 1204 Normandy was eventually conquered by the French. In the reign of which English king did this happen?

This castle at Bamburgh, Northumberland, has the square keep typical of Norman style.

What do you think 'Domesday' means?

Under the feudal system, peasants held land from the local lord's estate.

To work out the value of the vast lands he now held, in 1086 William sent agents to travel throughout England and make a record of all the villages and estates in the country. The information was collected together in the *Domesday Book*. This records a rural life that had changed little over the centuries. The population mainly worked on the land, although the lords of the manor were now French-speaking Normans, not Anglo-Saxon *thegns* The freedom of many of the peasants was reduced. For example, they had to ask the lord's permission for their daughters to get married.

William died in 1087 and was followed by his son, William Rufus. Direct **descendants** of William ruled England until 1154, when a related family, the Plantagenets, took power under Henry I. The royal household became more and more complicated, headed by a chancellor and other officers such as the earl marshal – positions that still exist today.

'After this had the king a large meeting, and very deep consultation with his council, about this land; how it was occupied, and by what sort of men. Then sent he his men over all England into each shire; commissioning them to find out how many hundreds of hides were in the shire, what land the king himself had, and what stock upon the land; or, what dues he ought to have by the year from the shire.'

Anglo-Saxon *Chronicle* entry for 1085 on the commissioning of the *Domesday Book*

This page of the *Domesday Book* lists estates, manors and villages in the county of Warwickshire.

How did the Normans build great castles and cathedrals?

The Normans were great builders, both in Normandy and, after the conquest, in England. They built massive stone castles and cathedrals that still stand today. Sometimes the building work lasted for decades.

Transporting and working in stone was difficult and expensive. At the **quarry** the stone was taken out by hammering iron wedges into the seam of stone to break off chunks, which were then sawn to the size needed. Most of the Norman buildings in the southeast of England and Normandy were constructed using stone from Normandy. Heavy stone had to be moved by boat, and so quarries near the coast or rivers were best. Once at the building site, materials were moved around on sledges, or, if lighter, in baskets. The lower layers of buildings were made from an inner core of rubble, with an outer face of ashlar – blocks of stone worked to give them a smoother finish. To raise stones to a higher level, a special form of crane operated by a wheel was used.

'So many smiths, carpenters, and other workmen were working so vehemently with bustle and noise that a man could scarcely hear the one next to him speaking.'

William FitzStephen, in his *Life of Thomas Becket*, the archbishop of Canterbury (c.1190)

🐾 Apart from the tall tower, what other defences does this castle have?

Rochester Castle in Kent is one of the best preserved Norman castles remaining in England. It was built in the 1120s.

DETECTIVE WORK

Why do you think the lengths of the walls on some Norman castles and cathedrals are different sizes? Why would one wall be slightly longer or shorter if it was measured by a different person?

These delicately carved pillars surround the cloister of the Norman cathedral at Monreale in Sicily.

A Norman drawing shows carpenters and masons hard at work on a new cathedral.

Building the largest castles and cathedrals would take many years. Before starting, the lines of the building were marked out on the ground. The distances were most often measured by walking and recording the number of feet paced. The construction was supervised by a master **mason**, a skilled craftsman who combined the roles of an **architect**, sculptor and builder. The stones, once placed, were smoothed off using an axe, or, for finer work, a chisel. The master mason would have been in charge of a team of craftsmen, including other masons and carpenters, since the roofs of the buildings were almost always made of a timber frame, finished off with thatch or tiles.

When the buildings were finished, the walls were often coated with plaster or whitewashed. This is how the great White Tower of the Tower of London got its name. Once finished, Norman buildings easily caught fire because of the material used in their roofs – in 1212 the authorities in London banned the use of straw or reeds to try to prevent this. Some Norman buildings were so poorly constructed that they simply fell down.

What is left of Norman England today?

Most of the buildings in **Norman England** would have been made of wood and so have long ago disappeared. Only the most important buildings, such as castles and churches, were built of stone. Many buildings became ruined over time and local people often removed the stone to build their own houses.

Within 20 years of the conquest, the Normans had built about 100 castles in England. The earliest type of castle was the **motte and bailey**. The motte was an artificial mound on which a wooden tower was built – often later replaced by a stone one – while the bailey was the building in which the castle's inhabitants lived. There are still some mottes surviving, such as at Berkhamstead in Hertfordshire. Later the Normans built stone keeps for their castles, with surrounding walls.

Unusually, this Norman house in Lincoln is built of stone. It is one of the oldest stone houses in Britain.

One of the best examples of this stage of Norman castle design is at Richmond in Yorkshire. The largest surviving Norman keeps are at the White Tower (part of the Tower of London) and Colchester Castle.

The Normans also built many stone churches and cathedrals in a style known as **Romanesque**. This was popular in the eleventh century. Romanesque churches had larger windows and doorways than Anglo-Saxon churches, with great arches and columns inside to support the weight of the building. Many of them had a great stone tower. The longest Norman cathedral was at Winchester, where the nave (the central section of the church) was about 180 m (590 ft) long. Other cathedral churches built in Norman times include Durham, St Albans, Norwich, Peterborough, Winchester, Hereford and Chichester.

The tower of Ely Cathedral is 30 m (100 ft) high.

Many surnames that are common today were originally Norman, such as Archer, Menzies, Graham, Morris and Knight. Some Norman customs survive, too. In the Channel Islands, the queen is still known as the 'duke of Normandy' as the islands are the last part of the old duchy of Normandy to be ruled by the English crown. When a bill is passed in the British Parliament, it is sent to the queen for her Royal Assent, or approval. She indicates her approval by writing '*La Reine le veult*', which is Norman French for 'The Queen wishes it so'.

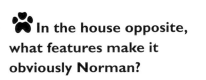 **In the house opposite, what features make it obviously Norman?**

The rounded arches of Norman churches allowed them to have wider doors and sturdier structures than Anglo-Saxon buildings.

Your project

The Normans have left many great castles and cathedrals, especially in England and Wales. Often we know the names of the great lords who lived in the castles, or the bishops and archbishops who ordered the cathedrals to be built.

Topic questions
● Are there any castles in your area that were built in Norman times? When were they built and what were the names of the Norman nobles who lived there? (If there are none in your area, choose a Norman castle from somewhere else.)

● Are there any Norman churches in your area? When were they built? Can you find the names of the priests/vicars from that time? Do their names sound English or French?

● Visit a Norman castle or church and draw a plan of the building. Which parts of it are from Norman times and which parts were added later? Is there a part that is Anglo-Saxon?

The Norman tower of St Alban's Cathedral dates from 1077 and was built by a bishop known as Paul of Caen.

● Look for your area in the *Domesday Book* on: http://www. nationalarchives.gov.uk/documentsonline/domesday.asp Have any of the place names survived today? How have the names changed?

The Tower of London was begun by William
the Conqueror in about 1078.

Project presentation
- Research your project well. Use the Internet and libraries
  to find out about the Normans and Anglo-Saxons.

- Tell the story of 1066 and the Norman Conquest from
  the point of view of either a Norman or an Anglo-Saxon.

- What was it like crossing the English Channel in boats
  and landing at Pevensey?

- How did it feel to march all the way to York to defeat
  Harald Hardrada and then back down south again?

- What did you do after the Anglo-Saxons lost the battle?

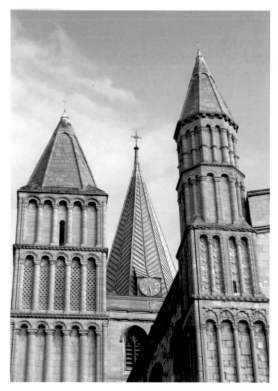

**The Norman cathedral in Rochester, Kent,
was built over an older Anglo-Saxon church.**

Glossary

architect A person who designs a building.

cavalry Soldiers who fight from horseback.

charge To rush forward suddenly to attack someone.

circa (shortened to c.) Used when dates are only approximately known.

conquest The taking of a kingdom by force.

count A man appointed by a king to rule over an area of land called a county.

crusades A series of expeditions by Christian knights to the Holy Land (modern-day Israel, Lebanon and Syria).

descendants The children, grandchildren and so on, of a person.

earl A powerful noble in Anglo-Saxon times.

exile Living abroad because it is not possible to return home.

fealty A special type of oath, by which a person promises to be loyal to a noble.

feudal system A system of society in which nobles received land from the king in return for military service.

heir A person who will take on the property or title of another person (often a parent) after their death.

hostage A prisoner who will only be released if a condition, such as paying money, is met.

interlock To overlap, for instance, shields, so that there are no gaps.

keep The tower of a castle.

mace A weapon with a metal ball at the end of a short pole.

mason A craftsman who is skilled at working in stone.

monasteries Places where a group of religious men, or monks, live together.

motte and bailey A type of castle with an inner fort (or keep) built on a mound called a motte, and an outer area, called a bailey.

noble A person from a family with a high status.

oath A special promise to behave in a particular way, often made on the Bible.

overthrow To remove someone (such as a king) from power by force.

pilgrimage A journey to a shrine or other sacred place.

quarry A place from which stone is cut.

rally To gather together ready for battle.

rebellion To organise a group to defy a government or authority.

reign The period of a king's or a queen's rule.

revolt To rise up against a figure of authority, such as the king.

Romanesque A style of building with round arches and large columns.

thegn A noble of less importance than an earl in Anglo-Saxon times.

vassal A person who swears fealty and receives land in return.

Answers

Page 5: He also wears a steel helmet and carries a shield.
Page 7: He holds a sceptre, which is a symbol of royalty.
Page 9: It is a reliquary, which is a box containing the bones of a saint. This would have made Harold's oath more sacred and binding.
Page 11: Before the arrival of Christianity, goods and valuables were buried with a person for use in the next life.
Page 13: They often cooked inside the hut in winter to heat it.
Page 14: They were dragons' heads. Sometimes a fire was lit beneath the head so that smoke came from the dragon's mouth to frighten people on the coast.
Page 16: They shot into the air so that the arrows would fall down like rain on the enemy, rather than just hitting the first row.
Page 19: Arrows could penetrate chain mail and even plate armour at the joins between plates.
Page 20: They are making an interlocking shield wall.
Page 22: The name comes from the old English word for 'doom'. 'Domesday' means day of judgement or reckoning. In other words, something that is being accounted for.
Page 24: The castle has an outer, defensive stone wall, known as a curtain wall.
Page 27: The rounded arches over the windows and doorway are typical Norman features.

Further Information

Books to read
The History Detective Investigates: Anglo-Saxons by Neil Tonge (Wayland 2006)
Hastings 1066: The Fall of Saxon England by Christopher Gravett (Osprey 2000)
The Normans: Warrior Knights and their Castles by Christopher Gravett (Osprey 2006)

Websites
http://historyonthenet.com/Normans/normansmain.htm
http://www.britannia.com/history/monarchs/mon22.html
Note to parents and teachers: Every effort has been made by the publishers to ensure that these websites are suitable for children. However, because of the nature of the Internet, it is impossible to guarantee that the contents of these sites will not be altered. We strongly advise that Internet access is supervised by a responsible adult.

Places to visit
The Tower of London, Tower Hill, London EC3N 4AB
Durham Cathedral, The College, Durham DH1 3EQ
Battle Abbey, Battle, near Hastings, East Sussex TN33 0AD

Index

The History Detective Investigates

Castles
978 0 7502 6230 9

What is a castle?
What was a motte and bailey?
When was the first stone castle built?
Who built the Tower of London?
Why were castles built in circles?
Who lived inside a castle?
How did people who lived in castles have fun?
Why did the Crusaders build castles?
Why did Edward I build castles in Wales?
Did castles have architects?
Why were castles besieged?
Why did castle-building stop?
Your project

Monarchs
978 0 7502 6231 6

What is a monarch?
Who was the first king of England?
When did Scotland first have a king?
Who was the first Norman king?
Why does Wales have a prince?
What were the Wars of the Roses?
Why did Henry VIII marry six times?
Who united the crowns?
Why did a king lose his head?
When did the kings speak German?
Which monarch reigned the longest?
Why is the royal family named after a castle?
Your project

The Normans and the Battle of Hastings
978 0 7502 6228 6

Who were the Normans?
Who was Duke William of Normandy?
Why did the Normans want to invade England?
Who were the Anglo-Saxons?
What was life like in England in the year 1066?
What threats did the Anglo-Saxons face?
What happened in the Battle of Hastings?
What weapons were used in the battle?
What does the Bayeux Tapestry tell us about the battle?
What was England like under Norman rule?
How did the Normans build great castles and cathedrals?
What is left of Norman England today?
Your project

Weapons and Armour through the Ages
978 0 7502 6229 3

What weapons did ancient peoples fight with?
What weapons did an ancient Roman soldier use?
Why were people so afraid of the Vikings?
Why did medieval knights wear such heavy armour?
Why were Mongol bows and arrows so deadly?
How did weapons change after the invention of gunpowder?
Why was the Japanese samurai sword so special?
What were the winning weapons in the Battle of Waterloo?
Why were rifles so important in the US Civil War?
Which invention killed millions of soldiers in the First World War?
What kinds of weapons were used on D-Day?
What weapons do modern Special Forces use?
Your project